# HOW TO EAT SUSHI PROPERLY

# HOW TO EAT SUSHI PROPERLY

## Includes Chopstick Etiquette

By Rebecca Black

Celestial Arc Publishing

Copyright © 2019 Rebecca Black. All rights reserved. This book is not to be reproduced or shared without permission from Rebecca Black.

**Celestial Arc Publishing**

ISBN-13: 9781079569162

# CONTENTS

**Introduction** .................................................................................. 7
    Why Sushi Etiquette? ........................................................... 7

**Chapter One: The Basics** ........................................................ 9
    Insult the Chef? .................................................................... 10
    Etiquette, Procedures, and the "Whys" ...... **Error! Bookmark not defined.**
    Sushi and More Sushi ......................................................... 11
    Let's Eat! ............................................................................. 15

**Chapter Two: Chopstick Etiquette** ....................................... 17
    The Basics .......................................................................... 18
    Do (s) and Don't (s) ........................................................... 18

**Your Author** ............................................................................ 23

# INTRODUCTION

## WHY SUSHI ETIQUETTE?

To those who love sushi, stating that it is popular is stating the obvious. Obvious and true. It is especially popular, not only in the U.S., but in many parts of the world. It is consumed on dates, the quick lunch, and more importantly during business meals. Therefore, I felt compelled to write a short, but concise chapter on the etiquette of eating sushi. Additionally, another factor was the numerous appeals from clients for just such a resource.

Of course, considering the etiquette of eating sushi, it may be best to also read the following chapter on chopstick etiquette.

Enjoy your sushi!

# CHAPTER ONE
# THE BASICS

# INSULT THE CHEF?

Sushi etiquette is evolving quite quickly; so quickly, in fact, that there are few non-debatable absolutes. Some heartily believe in mixing wasabi with the soy sauce, while some argue it insults the abilities of the chef. We will explore this subject and even more interesting discrepancies as we move forward.

Let's begin at the beginning: deciding where to sit when entering a sushi restaurant. Sitting at the sushi bar is quite a treat and requires just a bit more etiquette than if seated at a table. For example, if wishing to use the most proper etiquette, it is expected to ask those seated if the seats are available. This is most respectful to those seated. Moreover, since he/she is working at the counter, it is also most proper to consider what may or may not insult the sushi chef or itamae. More on this later.

# ETIQUETTE, PROCEDURES, AND THE "WHYS"

Most sushi is finger food, but many westerners use chopsticks. Both methods are fine but should be done correctly. Because it is viewed as a finger food, a towel (oshibori) is presented to the diner to clean the hands. Fold it back neatly after using. You may leave it to the left, next to the plate for finger wiping.

In front of each diner is a little cup or saucer for soy sauce of which it is impolite to fill fully. Fill no more than one third. More appears wasteful and disrespectful to the chef, as if he/she isn't capable of seasoning properly. This is very important to note when sitting at the sushi counter where the chef is in full view of the diner's actions.

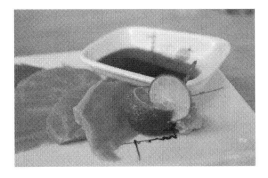

Sashimi is typically served first and is eaten with chopsticks. Most agree that a bit of wasabi should or could be added to the soy sauce for the sashimi, of which it is dipped. However, when sitting at the counter, it may be insulting to the chef. Therefore, adding a bit of wasabi to the meat first and then dipping in the sauce might be best.

Adding the wasabi to the sauce is in direct contrast to what some believe is proper for sushi eating. Some firmly believe that it is disrespectful and unnecessary to mix wasabi into the soy sauce, while some drone on and on about it being the only way to enjoy it, as if sushi wouldn't taste as good without *extra* wasabi.

This is the key here. If one enjoys more wasabi than is typically found in sushi, it is most polite to ask the chef to add more into the rolls or pieces. However, if one absolutely needs more wasabi, it is viewed as most polite to add a bit to the roll. If adding it to the soy sauce, it should be a very small amount.

# SUSHI AND MORE SUSHI

Not all sushi is created equal. There are absolute differences in quality, but for the sake of this little ditty, types are most important to discuss here, because there is a slightly different etiquette involved with each.

Nigiri (seasoned rice topped with fish or another topping) may be dipped in sauce—fish side down. However, if it has a glaze on it, it has already been seasoned. It is appropriate, though, to take some of the ginger (always served with sushi as a palette cleanser), dip it into the sauce with chopsticks, and brush the nigiri with it.

Gunkan (small cups made of sushi rice and dried seaweed which is filled with seafood or other ingredients) may be treated the same or soy sauce may be poured over it. The same goes for the taco or cone version of sushi: temaki.

Of course, the popular sushi roll westerners tend to enjoy, norimaki, or inside out sushi, is dipped using chopsticks.

With seasoned, glazed nigiri, no soy sauce is needed.

# LET'S EAT!

Now, on to eating sushi. If using the fingers, pick up a piece of nigiri with the index finger at the short side farthest from you and middle finger along the long side, so your palm would be "over" the sushi and the thumb on the opposite long side. Next< lift it up and flip it upside down. The fish is now on the bottom of the sushi and can be dipped into the soy sauce. Turn the wrist so that the fish is facing you.

Interestingly, it is considered perfect sushi eating to incline the head back and *somewhat* "toss" the piece in the mouth so that the fish is touching the tongue. This might take practice for some.

Although considered appropriate, for many of us these pieces are much too large to be eaten in one bite. What to do? If we bite it in half, it may fall apart. Of course, this might be the only choice if the bite really is too large for us. Nevertheless, there is nothing wrong with asking for the sushi to be made smaller. This is not an insult. However, this must be done before the sushi is made. If we do bite it in half, we hold onto the piece in between bites. It is not returned to the plate.

Using chopsticks to eat sushi is done similarly to using the fingers. Grip the nigiri firmly and turn it on its side (fish is pointing to the side); then while holding it sideways (one stick on the fish side and one on the rice side) turn the wrist so that the fish is facing down when dipping. A little bit of the rice may be dipped as well, but not much. It will fall apart.

# CHAPTER TWO
# CHOPSTICK ETIQUETTE

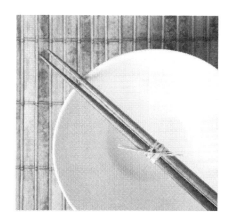

# THE BASICS

As we would never clean our hosts' utensils in their presence, the same is true of chopsticks. No rubbing them together.

Hold your chopsticks towards their end, not in the middle or the front third.

Place them parallel to yourself on the holder, with the tips to the left, (shoyu dish—most respectful) when not in use and return them to the original wrapper when finished with the meal.

If seated at a sushi bar, the chopsticks are placed parallel to the edge of the bar with the narrow ends on the chopstick rest or across your plate—never lean them on your plate.

The broad end is used to pick up sushi, or any other food, from a communal dish or to place food to another's dish. Never use the narrow ends that are used for eating to choose communal food to share.

Don't pass food from one set of chopsticks to another. This practice resembles a Japanese funeral ritual.

Never stick and leave chopsticks in food, especially rice, as it too resembles part of a funeral ritual.

These are not weapons. Do not spear or stab food with them. Additionally, never point, wave, play, or move dishes with them.

With large pieces of food, separate by cutting with the chopsticks: exert pressure in the center of the piece while tearing the two pieces apart. It is somewhat like a reverse scissors' movement. It is also acceptable to pick up the entire piece with your chopsticks and take a bite.

# DO (S) AND DON'T (S)

- Do ask what is freshest, but not if it is fresh.
- Do ask about specials or anything that may not be on the menu.
- Do not eat the ginger with the sushi. It is a palette cleanser to eat in between sushi pieces.
- Do not pour too much soy sauce in your dish.
- Do not disassemble sushi.
- When offered soup with no spoon, drink from the bowl. Guide the noodles to the mouth with chopsticks.
- Burping is impolite.
- Drink sake before or after the meal. The reasoning is that they are both rice products, thus don't mix well. Green tea or beer is thought to be a better accompaniment with sushi.
- Cold sake is higher quality than hot.
- When with others, pour drinks for them, as it is considered loutish to pour for oneself. Always watch their glasses and refill them. They will do the same. If they don't, finish the drink, and while holding the glass, lean it toward them slightly.
- Kanpai! (empty your cup) is the appropriate toast, but never use "chin-chin" as it refers to male genitalia.

- The itamae never touches money when handling food. The tip may be left in a jar, with wait staff, or on the bill.

*Knives and forks may be used in high-end western restaurants only if offered.*

# YOUR AUTHOR

Your author, Rebecca Black, also known as The Polite One, recently retired from her company **Etiquette Now!** after a successful and rewarding 20+ years. As the owner and facilitator of her company, this retired elementary school teacher designed and presented custom etiquette workshops for the individual, corporate, governmental and educational client. Due to her extensive knowledge of the subject, she is also a well-respected author of etiquette books and lesson plans.

Considered an expert in the field, Rebecca answers etiquette questions (Q & A) and offers advice through her blogs: Got Etiquette Advice, Got Wedding Etiquette, and The Polite One's Insights.

Although for many years, Rebecca, focused her writing on etiquette issues, she is currently following her passion of writing fiction. A few of her most recent children's books also focus on the environment: *Save the Jellywonkers: Help Keep The Oceans Clean; Beware the Blackness, A Jellywonker Adventure;* and *The Tale of a Bear & Pony: A Yellowstone Adventure*

Please visit rebeccablackauthor.blogspot.com for more information about Rebecca's current news.

### Connect with Us
https://www.facebook.com/ThePoliteOne
https://www.facebook.com/rebeccablackauthor/

### Visit Us
Rebecca Black Author

Etiquette Now! Insights

Got Etiquette Advice

Got Wedding Etiquette

Living Well & Enjoying Life—Rebecca Style

The Polite One's Insights

The Polite Traveler

https://www.amazon.com/author/rebecca_black

### Published Fiction Books by Rebecca Black
*The Tale of a Bear & Pony; A Yellowstone Adventure*

*Save The Jellywonkers! -- Help Keep Our Oceans Clean*

*Beware the Blackness! A Jellywonker Adventure*

*Sapphire and the Atlantians*

*War in Atlantis*

*The Return of the Tui Suri*

## Published Etiquette Books by Rebecca Black

*Dining Etiquette: Essential Guide for Table Manners, Business Meals, Sushi, Wine and Tea Etiquette*

*Dress for All Occasions—The Basics, Attire Must-Haves, Dress Code Definitions & FAQs*

*Entertaining Skills 101: Lesson Plans for Those Who Wish to Present Workshops*

*Etiquette for the Important Events in Our Lives: Common sense etiquette with a side of history and a dollop of gift-giving savvy*

*Etiquette for the Socially Savvy Adult: Life Skills for All Situations*

*Etiquette for the Socially Savvy Teen: Life Skills for All Situations*

*Golf Etiquette: Civility on the Course*

*How to Tea: British Tea Times*

*How to Teach Your Children Manners: Essential Life Skills Your Child Needs to Know!*

*International Business Travel Etiquette: Seal the Deal by Understanding Proper Protocol*

*Reaching Your Potential: How to use our life lessons to grow as a person and to improve the workplace environment*

*Societal Rage: Problem solving for our increasingly violent world*

*Sushi Etiquette: The guide for those who wish to eat sushi properly and avoid insulting the chef*

*Train the Trainer Guide: The essential guide for those who wish to present workshops and classes for adults*

*Wedding & Reception Planning: The Etiquette Guide for Planning the Perfect Wedding*

*Wine Etiquette--From holding the glass to ordering a bottle of wine in a restaurant and everything in-between*

*Workplace Etiquette: How to Create a Civil Workplace*

## Published Lesson Plans

*Business Meal Etiquette*

*Career Fair Etiquette*

*Entertaining Skills 101*

*Etiquette for the Socially Savvy Teen*

*Golf Etiquette*

*Growing Up Socially Savvy*

*How to Become a Socially Savvy Lady*

*How to Tea; British Tea Times*

*How to Teach Your Children Manners*

*Just for Teens, Skills for the Socially Savvy*

*Manners for Children*

*Organizational Skills*

*Prom Etiquette*

*Proper Business Attire*

*Skills for the Socially Savvy and Well-Dressed Teen*

*Skills for the Socially Savvy and Well-Organized Teen*

*Table Manners*

*Train the Trainer*

*Wine Etiquette*

*Workplace Etiquette*

**Wedding Lesson Plans**

*Lessons for the Newly Engaged*

*Wedding Planning*

*Wedding Reception Planning*

Please visit https://www.amazon.com/author/rebecca_black for information about collecting more etiquette books.

Printed in Great Britain
by Amazon